Learning to read. Reading to learn!

LEVEL ONE Sounding It Out Preschool–Kindergarten
For kids who know their alphabet and are starting to sound out words.

learning sight words • beginning reading • sounding out words

LEVEL TWO Reading with Help Preschool–Grade 1
For kids who know sight words and are learning to sound out new words.

expanding vocabulary • building confidence • sounding out bigger words

LEVEL THREE Independent Reading Grades 1–3
For kids who are beginning to read on their own.

introducing paragraphs • challenging vocabulary • reading for comprehension

LEVEL FOUR Chapters Grades 2–4
For confident readers who enjoy a mixture of images and story.

reading for learning • more complex content • feeding curiosity

Ripley Readers Designed to help kids build their reading skills and confidence at any level, this program offers a variety of fun, entertaining, and unbelievable topics to interest even the most reluctant readers. With stories and information that will spark their curiosity, each book will motivate them to start and keep reading.

Vice President, Licensing & Publishing Amanda Joiner
Editorial Manager Carrie Bolin

Editor Jordie R. Orlando
Designer Luis Fuentes
Reprographics Bob Prohaska

Chief Executive Officer Andy Edwards
Chief Commercial Officer Brett Clarke
**Vice President, Global Licensing &
    Consumer Products** Cassie Dombrowski
Vice President, Creative Dov Ribnik
Director, Brand & Athlete Marketing Ricky Melnik
**Account Manager, Global Licensing &
    Consumer Products** Andrew Hogan
Athlete Manager Chris Haffey
Special Thanks Vicki Golden

PHOTO CREDITS

NITRO CIRCUS

STAY GOLDEN

FEATURING:

VICKI GOLDEN

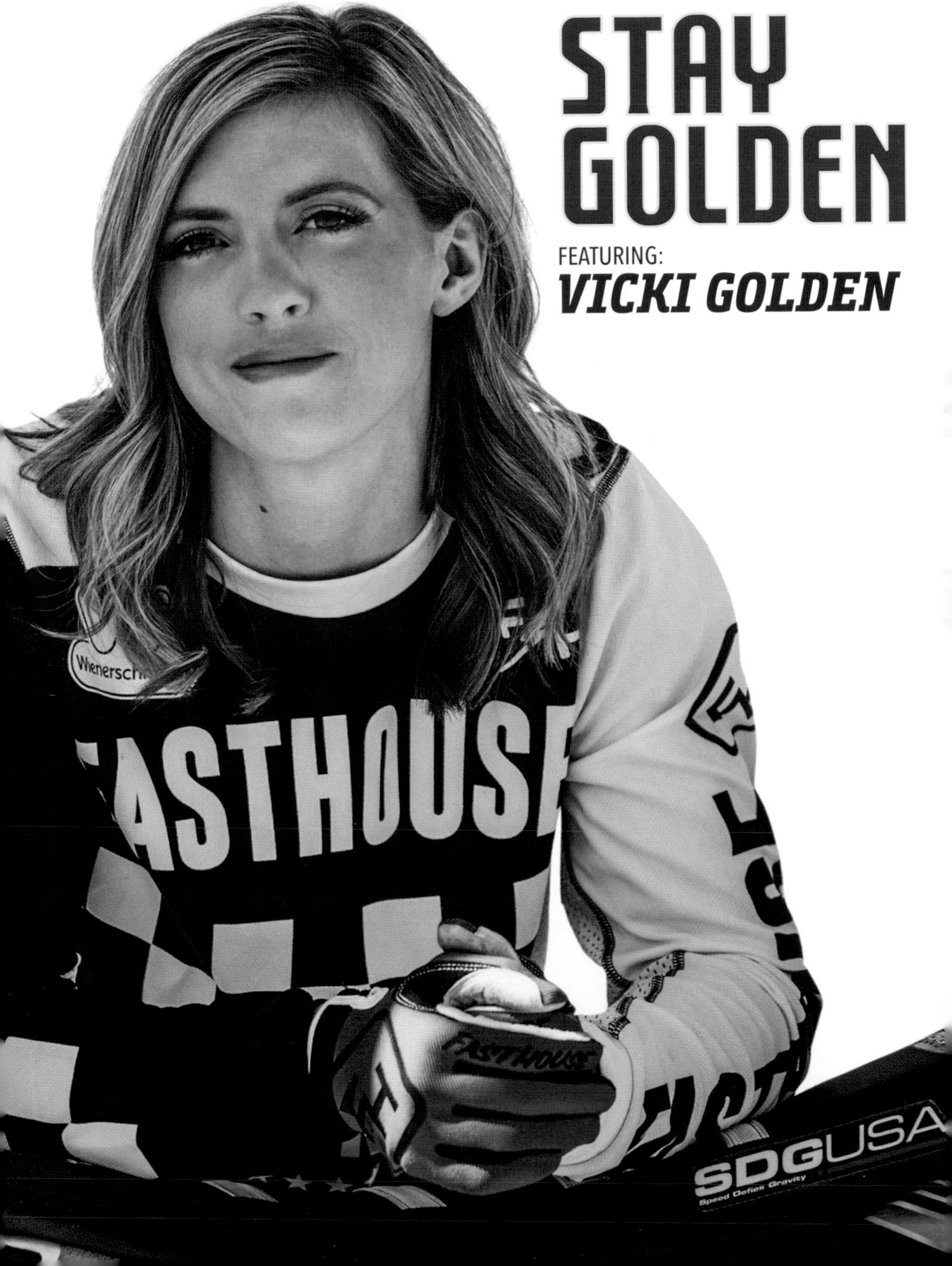

Riding motorcycles is Vicki
Golden's favorite thing to do!

She rides motorcycles in
shows with Nitro Circus.

Vicki's motto is "Never quit!"

When she was young, Vicki's parents told her that quitting can become a bad habit. She says, "I've made it a habit *not* to quit. I don't know how to quit."

When Vicki was seven years old, her older brother got a dirt bike. She watched him learn how to ride and do tricks. Vicki wanted to ride, too!

After asking her parents over and over, Vicki got her own dirt bike. She has been riding ever since.

Vicki does a special type
of motorcycle riding called
freestyle motocross, or FMX.
FMX riders drive on dirt tracks
and jump off of ramps to do
cool stunts.

Vicki has been a professional
motocross rider since she was
16 years old!

Vicki has accomplished a lot as an FMX rider. Even when people told her she couldn't achieve something, she proved them wrong.

She never quits!

Vicki was the first woman
to compete in an X Games
FMX competition.

The X Games are where some of the best action sports athletes go to see who can do the hardest tricks.

Riders have to show judges they are good enough to compete in the X Games.

Vicki was very sick the first time she had to show off her skills. She was so good, the judges still picked her to ride in the X Games!

Vicki is also one of the first women to compete in Supercross and Arenacross races.

These kinds of races are held on narrow dirt tracks built inside stadiums.

Some people think that because Vicki is a woman, she can't ride as well as the men riders. Her three X Games gold medals prove them wrong!

There are still times when Vicki doubts herself. It is normal for people to fail before reaching big goals.

Vicki always keeps trying. She says, "If I have a goal, it's going to happen sooner or later!"

Vicki does not let anything get in her way. Not long after recovering from a bad injury, she landed a backflip off of a Moon Booter ramp! She was the first female FMX athlete to ever do this!

In 2019, she rode her motorcycle through 13 flaming wooden walls!

Be careful, Vicki!

But what Vicki loves most
is riding with her friends.

She says, "There's nothing better than when you get a good group together and go ride."

Never quit!

Ripley Readers

Ready for More?

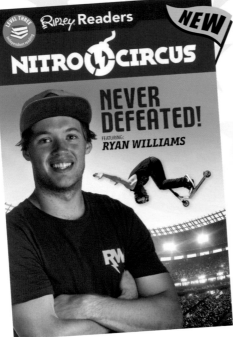

Ripley Readers — LEVEL THREE Independent readers

NITRO CIRCUS — **NEW**

NEVER DEFEATED!
FEATURING: RYAN WILLIAMS

NEVER DEFEATED!

FEATURING:
RYAN WILLIAMS

Meet the amazing athletes of Nitro Circus and find out just what inspires them to be the best!

Appropriate for grades 1–3, this Level 3 Ripley Reader introduces award-winning athlete Ryan Williams. Featuring his lifelong love of scooter and BMX, favorite achievements, and more, kids will love learning about Ryan and his inspiring attitude— **Never Defeated!**

Learning to read. Reading to learn!

LEVEL TWO — Reading with help

Reading With Help
Preschool–Grade 1
- expanding vocabulary
- building confidence
- sounding out bigger words

LEVEL THREE — Independent reading

Independent Readin
Grades 1–3
- introducing paragraphs
- challenging vocabulary
- reading for comprehens

For more information about
Ripley's Believe It or Not!, go to www.ripleys.com